Contents

Name ....

KEY STAGE 2 NATIONAL TESTS: HOW THEY WORK

Pupils between the ages of 7 and 11 (Years 3–6) cover Key Stage 2 of the National Curriculum. In May of their final year of Key Stage 2 (Year 6), all pupils take written National Tests (commonly known as SATs) in the three most important subjects: English, Mathematics and Science. The tests are carried out in school, under the supervision of teachers, but are marked by examiners outside the school.

The tests help to find out what children have learned in the key subjects. They will also help parents and teachers to know whether children are reaching the national standards set out in the National Curriculum.

Each child will probably spend in total around $4\frac{1}{2}$ hours during one week in May sitting the tests. In Mathematics and Science most children will do two papers, and three in English. The tests provide a summative 'snapshot' of pupils' work in tasks which have been standardised through pre-testing. Teacher assessment is based on the full range of pupils' work in relation to the Programmes of Study.

The school sends the papers away to external examiners for marking. After being marked, the papers are returned to the school and results reported to parents by the end of July. With the results of the tests, you will also receive the results of assessments made by teachers in the classroom, based on the work your child has done during the school year. You will also receive a summary of the results for all pupils at the school, and for pupils nationally. This will help you to know how your child is doing compared with other children of the same age.

The report from your child's school will explain to you what the results show about your child's progress, strengths, particular achievements and targets for development. It will also explain how to follow up the results with your child's teachers and why the test results may be different from the teacher's assessment.

WHY THE KEY STAGE 2 NATIONAL TESTS ARE IMPORTANT

It is very important that children do as well as they can in their National Tests. Although the results should not be used by secondary schools to determine which children to give places to, they may be used in other ways. For example, the results could be used to determine which subject teaching group your child will be placed in. Good test results, together with a positive report from the primary school, may ensure your child is placed in a higher group.

LEVELS OF ACHIEVEMENT: KNOWING HOW WELL YOUR CHILD IS DOING

The National Curriculum divides each subject into a number of levels, from one to eight. On average, children are expected to advance one level for every two years they are at school. It is reasonable to expect that, by the end of Key Stage 2, most children should be between Levels 3 and 5. Some children might reach Level 6, and this should be recognised as an excellent result. The following table includes the levels for 7-, 11- and 14-year-olds (for the end of Key Stages 1, 2 and 3) to give you an overall picture of how your child should progress.

	7 years	11 years	14 years
Above Level 8			Exceptional performance
Level 8			Exceeded targets
Level 7			Exceeded targets
Level 6		Exceptional performance	Achieved targets
Level 5		Exceeded targets	Achieved targets
Level 4	Exceptional performance	Achieved targets	Working towards
Level 3	Exceeded targets	Working towards	Working towards
Level 2	Achieved targets	Working towards	Working towards
Level 1	Working towards	Working towards	Working towards

Legend:

- ☐ Exceptional performance
- ▨ Exceeded targets for age group
- ▢ Achieved targets for age group
- ▩ Working towards targets for age group

Your child compared with his or her age group

There are different Key Stage 2 National Tests for different ability levels. This is to ensure that pupils can take a test paper where they can show positive achievement, and not be discouraged by trying to answer questions which are too easy or too difficult. Most children will take the three papers for Levels 3–5 in English. The tests take the following amounts of time: the Reading and Writing Tests both take 70 minutes and the Spelling and Handwriting Test takes 15 minutes. Additionally, from 1996, there will be an extension paper lasting for 60 minutes for candidates aiming at Level 6. Level 6 can only be awarded if Level 5 has been achieved in the Level 3–5 papers.

This book concentrates on Levels 3–5, giving plenty of practice to achieve the best level possible. It also provides sufficient rigour to enable children to attempt the extension paper. If your child can reach Level 5 having done the main questions, then your child will already be above the average for his or her age. The table below shows you what percentage of pupils nationally reached each of the levels in the 1994 tests for English.

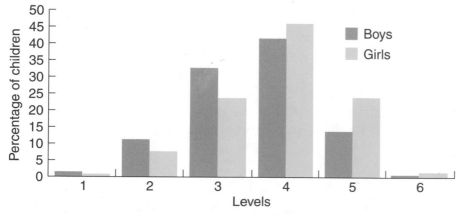

Levels achieved in English, 1994

Preparing and practising for the National Tests

ENGLISH AT KEY STAGE 2

The questions in this book will help you prepare your child by testing him or her on the Key Stage 2 curriculum for English. For assessment purposes, the current National Curriculum divides English into three sections, called Attainment Targets (ATs). The first AT, Speaking and Listening, is assessed only by the teacher in the classroom, not in the written tests. The other two ATs are:

AT2: Reading

AT3: Writing

The English National Curriculum defines level descriptions for each of the three ATs. These are taken together to give an overall level for English. The test papers have questions covering each of these ATs. Spelling and Handwriting are tested separately from Writing.

USING THIS BOOK TO HELP YOUR CHILD PREPARE FOR THE NATIONAL TEST IN ENGLISH

This book contains four basic features:

Questions:	test papers in Reading, Writing and Spelling and Handwriting
Answers:	showing acceptable responses and marks
Information to the Parent:	giving advice to help improve your child's score and ensure that common mistakes are not made
Level chart:	showing you how to interpret your child's marks to arrive at a level.

Details of how to run the tests at home are given below. Information about how to mark the tests and assess your child can be found on page 51.

In the margin of each question page, there are small boxes. These are divided in half, with the marks available for that question at the bottom, and a blank at the top for you to fill in your child's score.

SIMULATING TEST CONDITIONS

Allow 1 hour and 10 minutes each for the Reading Test and the Writing Test. The Spelling and Handwriting Test is likely to take 15 minutes. Let your child carry out the test in a place where he or she is comfortable. Allow your child to do these three tests on separate occasions. Set the Reading Test first, preferably on a different day from the other two. Allow a break (for example, lunchtime) between the Writing Test and the Spelling and Handwriting Test.

Detailed requirements of timings and the way to approach each test can be found on page 1 (the Reading Test), page 12 (the Writing Test) and page 19 (the Spelling and Handwriting Test). Provide a clock, enabling your child to complete the starting and finishing times at the beginning of the tests.

MARKING THE QUESTIONS

Guidance on how to mark your child's answers to the questions is given with each section. See the Contents page.

FINALLY, AS THE TESTS DRAW NEAR

In the days before the tests, make sure your child is as relaxed and confident as possible. You can help by encouraging your child to believe in him or herself and the teacher! Remind your child of the need to concentrate but to minimise tension – encourage him or her to *enjoy* these tests.

Look out for signs of anxiety, such as changes in eating or sleeping habits. Although many children look forward to tests, it is only natural that some may be nervous. Reassure your child that, though very important, the tests are not the only means by which he or she will be assessed.

A parent's guide to the Reading Test

To answer the questions in the Reading Test your child must first read the magazine 'Young and Old' at the end of this booklet. Detach it carefully and staple or clip it together. Now read through these instructions and the Information for the Parent on page 22. Make sure you are thoroughly familiar with what your child will be working on.

Introduce your child to the magazine and briefly summarise the four sections of writing in it.

Now ask your child to turn to where the story 'Rescuing Gloria' begins on page 1 of the magazine. Read out the short instructions on page 2 of this book and explain that he or she has 20 minutes to read through the magazine and after this will have to answer questions about it.

Allow your child 20 minutes to read quietly, and fairly quickly. If your child finishes the story, he or she should carry on through the magazine. When the 20 minutes have elapsed, ask your child to stop reading. Reassure him or her that there is no need to worry if he or she has not finished reading everything in the magazine.

Your child needs the magazine and the Reading Test section (pages 3–11) as he or she works through the test.

Now read aloud the example question on page 2 with your child and help him or her to answer it correctly.

In your own words describe how your child should work through the test, making sure to include these points:

- Wherever the pencil symbol appears an answer must be written.

- If a question is too hard, your child should go on to the next one.

- He or she may look at the magazine as often as needed when answering the questions.

- After finishing a page he or she should turn over to a new page without waiting to be told.

- Marks will not be given for spelling, handwriting, punctuation or grammar in this part of the English test.

- There are 50 minutes to complete this test.

Note the starting time in the appropriate place on page 3. When 50 minutes have elapsed ask your child to stop. Note the finishing time in the appropriate place.

When you have completed the marking add up the marks to give a Reading Test Total, and enter this in the box provided on page 11. You will need this total mark when finding your child's KS2 level on page 51.

1

Instructions

The questions in this section are about the contents of your magazine: the story, the information piece about 'Good Neighbours', the poem and 'Bookshelf'.

Your parent will explain how you are to do the first task by going through the following example with you.

As your parent reads the example aloud you will see four possible answers. In each case choose the best word, or group of words, to fit the passage and put a ring round it.

You may look at the magazine as often as you wish when you are answering the questions.

GOOD LUCK!

Example

The title of this magazine is

On the Road   Forever Friends   (Rescuing Gloria)   Alone Again

and the story is about a

(goat)   sports car   cuckoo clock   gerbil

Now please wait until your parent tells you to start work on page 3 in the same way.

When you have finished page 3 you should turn over the page and carry on working through to the end of the reading section of this book (page 11).

About the story   Questions 1–9

Start

Finish

1   At the start of the story Leo glared through the

door   window   mirror   mist .

2   He was unhappy. He wished he lived near

rats and mice   cows and pigs   cats and dogs   ducks and geese .

3   Leo let himself out of the house quietly because he didn't want to

meet somone his own age   wake baby Alice   spot the girl in the flat   get caught by someone old .

4   Leo spent time outside the window where a girl was watering plants because he

wanted her to notice him   already knew her   liked nature   thought she was lonely .

5   He stopped beside a battered

Transit van   phone-box   Land Rover   litter bin .

6   When Leo met Harjinder he thought she seemed

friendly   bad-mannered   cheeky   unhelpful .

7   When the goat let go of his jacket Leo was

disappointed   amazed   unhappy   sad .

8   The old man was getting rid of Gloria because

he was fed up with her   she was ill   he was losing his land   Leo liked her .

but Leo knew a place where she could live!

Letts

Q1 **1**

Q2 **1**

Q3 **1**

Q4 **1**

Q5 **1**

Q6 **1**

Q7 **1**

Q8 **1**

2

Q9

What happens in the story?

9 Here are some of the events that have happened in the story so far. Put all these events in the right order by numbering each line. The first event has been numbered for you.

.... Leo stops by a Land Rover.

.... Leo meets the old man who owns Gloria.

.... Leo hears a new baby scream worse than Alice.

....1.... Leo moves to a new home.

.... Harjinder rescues Leo.

.... Leo spots the girl watering plants.

.... A goat tugs Leo's jacket.

About the characters   Questions 10–16

The main *human* character in the story is Leo. Some parts of the story tell you a lot about what kind of person he is.

Look at these extracts from the story. In the space opposite each one, write what it tells you about Leo's character. The first one has been done for you.

Extract from the story	What it tells you about Leo's character
Great-grannies and great-*great*-grandads! He hadn't seen anyone under a hundred and fifty since they had moved in. He stamped angrily through the sitting room and glared at the view through his bedroom window instead.	Leo is unhappy about living in an area with so many old people. He seems to be rather intolerant and bad-tempered.

4

10 Oh, that was *really* wonderful, wasn't it! At last he'd found someone his own age – and all she cared about was plants! His smile faded and he felt awkward and stupid.

11 Suddenly, the words made a picture in Leo's head. The picture of the spare piece of ground that was overgrown and tangled. *Gloria could live in the wild garden next door.*

12 We also meet Harjinder. Look at this extract from the story. In the space write what it tells you about Harjinder's character.

Extract from the story	What it tells you about Harjinder's character
She looked carefully at the goat and then she gave him a grin. Friendly and calm ... Tipping the carrots on to the rest of the shopping she held out the paper bag.	

13 When Leo stopped beside the Land Rover he wanted to scream. Why?

....

....

14 How can the old man tell that Gloria likes Leo?

....

....

Letts

2
Q15

15 Why doesn't Leo want to explain exactly where he lives?

....

....

2
Q16

16 At the start of the story Leo seems to dislike old people. Do you think this dislike is as strong as it seems?

Yes ☐   No ☐

What in the story suggests this?

....

....

....

....

....

How the story is written   Questions 17–21

2
Q17

17 In the first paragraph of the story the writer makes it clear that Leo is not happy about moving to the new flat.

Find five different words which she uses to show his feelings.

☐   ☐   ☐

☐   ☐

1
Q18

18 The writer gives a vivid picture of the flat with all the pot plants.

Find three words which describe this vegetation.

☐   ☐   ☐

6

19 The old man says that Gloria has 'got a bad case of the motorways'.

Explain what he means.

1
Q19

....

....

....

20 Gloria's owner tells Leo that the goat is going to be put to sleep.

What one word does the writer use to show the old man's anger and bitterness?

1
Q20

Your opinion   Questions 21–22

21 Would you be interested in reading the rest of this story?

Yes [   ]   No [   ]

3
Q21

Say what you liked or did not like about the part you have read so far.

....

....

....

22 You have read only the first part of Leo's story.

What do you think that the rest of the story might be about?

Why do you think so?

2
Q22

....

....

....

About the article   Questions 1–4

1 Write down **THREE** things which the children do to help the old people.

(i) ....

(ii) ....

(iii) ....

2 How did Sarah and her friends first meet their elderly neighbours?

....

....

3 When we read the article we can guess the reporter's opinion about the 'Good Neighbours' scheme. What is her opinion?

....

....

....

4 Write out **ONE** sentence or phrase that shows what she thinks about their work.

....

....

The opinions of the letter writers   Questions 1–4

5 Both Martin and Jane wrote a P.S. at the end of their letters but these were not printed in the magazine. Which one wrote:

P.S. I hope the excellent links between the generations will continue when the children go to High School.

1 Q1(i)

1 Q1(ii)

1 Q1(iii)

1 Q2

2 Q3

1 Q4

P.S. Isn't school about learning about Maths, Science and English, rather than visiting the elderly?

1
Q5

6 Look again at Martin's points. He is saying that pets are often dirty and can cause bad health.

a In what way does he think that they can be dirty?

1
Q6a

....

....

b In what way does Martin think that they could be bad for people's health?

1
Q6b

....

....

7a Look again at the letter from Jane. Who does she think will welcome her School/Home Watch plan?

1
Q7a

....

b Why might the scheme be welcome?

1
Q7b

....

....

8 Which letter do you agree with? Jane's or Martin's? Perhaps you have a different point of view.

2
Q8

Write down what *you* think about the article and say why.

....

....

....

....

9

About the poem   Questions 1–5

1 Why is Johnny Armstrong described as being like a question mark?

1
Q1

....

....

....

2 How has Benwell changed during Johnny's life?

1
Q2

....

....

....

3 In verse four, what does the poet's choice of the word 'cell' tell you about Johnny's life?

1
Q3

....

....

....

4 Why, do you think, does Johnny go to the park day after day?

2
Q4

....

....

....

5 What are your feelings about Johnny Armstrong's life, now that he is eighty or more?

2
Q5

....

....

....

6 Re-read this extract from the poem.

> O the wind in park trees is
> the self-same wind
> That first blew on a village child
> When life freshly unfurled in
> a green, lost world
> And his straight limbs ran wild.

There are many 's' sounds in these lines. What effect do they have?

....

....

....

Using the Bookshelf   Questions 1 and 2

1 Look at page 12 of the magazine.

You are asked to imagine that you are choosing books for some of the characters from the story 'Rescuing Gloria'.

Which book might you choose for the following people? The first one has been done for you.

(i) Leo's mum ...The Complete Book of Mother and Baby Care...

(ii) His sister Alice ....

(iii) The girl watering plants ....

(iv) The old man ....

(v) Leo ....

2 The books on the list are of two main sorts. What are these?

(i)...

....

....

(ii) ....

	Reading Test Score
'Rescuing Gloria'	
'Good Neighbours'	
'Old Johnny Armstrong'	
'Bookshelf'	
READING TEST TOTAL	

Explain to your child that he or she is going to write a story or description on his or her own and within a time limit. Before doing this there will be some time to plan it, preparing some notes which he or she can refer to during the writing session. Emphasise that he or she is writing a short story or a brief episode from a story or a description, not a long chapter from a novel.

Allow five or ten minutes to talk with your child about interesting short stories or descriptions which he or she may have read or written recently. You may wish to focus on the extract from 'Rescuing Gloria' and, for descriptive writing, 'Old Johnny Armstrong'. This discussion should revise your child's awareness of:

IN A SHORT STORY

- beginning in a way that captures the reader's attention;

- the importance of initiating the action and setting the plot in motion quickly in a short story;

- a manageable number of characters who can be developed using comments, description and dialogue (conversation);

- continuing in a way that makes the reader interested in what happens next;

- bringing the short story to a convincing conclusion.

IN A DESCRIPTION

- gaining and keeping the reader's attention;

- considering different aspects of the subject of the description;

- using a range of interesting descriptive vocabulary;

- making interesting comparisons;

- finishing the description in an interesting way.

Now read the general instructions on page 13 to your child. Go through the starting points together. Your child will choose the title which he or she thinks will make the best short story. Make sure your child understands how to plan the story, using the planning sheets on pages 15 and 16 or his or her own method of planning. Allow 15 minutes planning time for your child to think about what to write and to plan his or her story or description. If your child needs less planning time he or she can begin to write when ready.

Writing sheets are provided in this book on pages 17 and 18. Provide more A4 paper for your child if necessary. Allow 55 minutes for writing time. Enter the starting and finishing times in the appropriate places on page 17.

When you have finished the marking add up the marks to give a Writing Test Total and enter this in the box provided on page 18. You will need this total mark when finding your child's KS2 level on page 51.

Writing

Instructions

Here are some starting points for writing and two planning sheets to help you organise your ideas.

Your parent will go through each one of the starting points with you, and explain how to use the space for planning your writing before you start.

You will have 15 minutes in which to think about what to write and to jot down your ideas.

You will then have 55 minutes to complete your writing.

Choose **ONE** starting point. Then use the appropriate planning sheet on page 15 or 16 to help plan your writing.

Starting points

1 Making friends

Leo had moved to a new home and didn't know how to get people to talk to him. It isn't always easy to make friends.

Imagine someone goes to live somewhere new where he or she doesn't know anyone.

Write a short story about what happens. The person in the story may be you.

2 Future life

Imagine what your life will be like in the year 2050. You will be about seventy years old! Much may have happened to yourself and in the world about you.

Write a short story about your life. You may wish to tell your reader about:

- **what the world is like in the middle of the next century;**

- **your own way of life and family;**

- **your feelings at this time in your life.**

3 **Story starters**

'The house was empty, the mysterious garden a wild tangle inviting exploration.'

Write a short story about what happened when you explored the house and garden.

4 **An interesting old person**

The story and the poem both feature interesting old people.

EITHER:

Think of an older person known to yourself, for example a grandparent;

OR:

Make up an old person, using your knowledge of the lives of older people.

Write a description of this person and his or her way of life. Have you chosen ONE of the starting points? Now, make a note of some of your ideas. Jot them down on a piece of paper, or turn over and use one of the planning sheets.

Planning sheet (short story)

Which title have you chosen to write about?

I have got you

Setting

Characters (e.g. Who are they? What are they like?)

What makes the story begin?

What happens next?

How will your story end?

Planning sheet (personal description)

THE OLDER PERSON

His or her appearance	His or her life in the past
His or her life now	His or her character

Writing

....

....

....

....

....

....

....

....

....

....

....

....

....

....

....

....

....

....

....

....

....

....

....

....

....

....

....

....

....

....

....

....

....

....

Ask for more paper if you need it.

	Writing Test Score
Purpose and Organisation	
Grammar	
Style	
WRITING TEST TOTAL	

A parent's guide to the Spelling and Handwriting Test

This spelling test is likely to take 15 minutes.

In this test you will read the text of a story out loud to your child twice. Read it through the first time without stopping. Then read it aloud a second time, pausing in the appropriate places to allow your child to insert the missing words in his or her version of the story. The full text for your use is on page 46 and you can detach it if you wish. The words printed in bold italics are the words your child will have to spell. Your child's version of the story is on pages 20–21, with lines to complete in place of these words.

Encourage your child to make his or her best attempt at spelling even unfamiliar words. Allow sufficient time for each missing word to be written.

Read aloud the following instructions to your child. Adapt them or repeat them as you judge necessary.

- *I am going to read out a story called* 'Through Space in Eternity'. *I will read it twice.*

- *You will follow your version, which has words missing.*

- *Follow as I read through the passage for the first time. Don't write anything at this stage. I will then read it out again, giving you time to write the missing words in the gaps.*

Before the second reading tell your child:

- *I will now read the passage to you again.*

- *When you come to a gap wait for me to tell you the word and then write it in the space.*

- *If you are not sure how to spell it just have a go and write the letters you think are correct.*

Enter the starting and finishing times in the appropriate places.

Enter the score in the box provided on page 21. You will need this score when finding your child's KS2 level on page 51.

HANDWRITING

Allow five minutes for the handwriting test, which is on page 21.

In this test your child is asked to copy a few lines of the spelling test passage. Encourage him or her to do the best he or she can, but not to be too tense or to try too hard.

Enter the starting and finishing times in the appropriate places.

Enter the score in the box provided on page 21. You will need this score when finding your child's KS2 level on page 51.

Spelling and Handwriting

Through Space in 'Eternity'

Start _____
Finish _____

All around the Earth people .... on as

the .... rapidly ....

for the launch of United Nations' deep space craft *Eternity*.

   Their minds were .... on a billion virtual

.... sets. The .... of many lasers

.... the launch site, cutting the African night;

tension was mounting inside the command centre. After much

.... the time had come to explore space in the remote

control craft, seeking some .... on which human

life could be established.

   Why was this voyage taking place? By the year 2050 A.D. Earth

had become even more crowded. The population multiplied and

consumed at an ever-increasing rate. Human selfishness had

destroyed ...., now humanity itself was

threatened. It appeared that nothing .... prevent

an environmental disaster.

   The .... of the deep space craft was limited.

From a million volunteers from all over the ....

1 Q1
1 Q2   1 Q3
1 Q4
1 Q5   1 Q6
1 Q7
1 Q8
1 Q9
1 Q10
1 Q11
1 Q12
1 Q13

one hundred were .... chosen. Life on a new

planet would be difficult. Tolerance, intelligence and confidence

were particularly important qualities.

The journey they faced was long. Medical science knew how to

.... them, injections of ....

would stop bones from ...., artificial

.... replaced blood.

Many dangers lay ahead. Barring ....,

the travellers would reach their destination in 2150 A.D., having

slept for a ....!

1 Q14

1 Q15   **1** Q16

1 Q17

1 Q18

1 Q19

1 Q20

Spelling Score

Using your best joined-up writing, copy this last section on the lines
provided.

**Who could say how successful their journey might be?
Could this brave mission find a place for the human race,
somewhere deep in space?**

....

....

....

....

Handwriting
Score

Information for the parent
Reading at KS2: AT2

Effective teaching and learning at KS2 will have taken place when planned from the Programmes of Study for English and implemented in classrooms where talk, reading and writing are integrated. A wide variety of evidence about your child as a reader is available to his or her teacher; no test can identify and give a level to *any* reader's full range of achievements.

The KS2 reading test focuses on several elements from the Programmes of Study. It is designed to gather evidence about a child's ability to:

- read, understand and respond to a range of writing;

- understand and write about plot, setting, character and ideas in fiction;

- look at a text for details about character or action in order to draw conclusions, predict and make judgements;

- develop and express his or her own views and preferences, referring to details from a text to support his or her responses;

- use inference, deduction and previous reading experience to find and appreciate meanings beyond the literal;

- appreciate imaginative use of English and the effect of a writer's choice of words and phrases on the reader;

- select appropriate reference books;

- skim read;

- retrieve information.

Note to Parent

Before you mark your child's responses to the Reading Test do re-read the magazine. This will help you to clarify the information in the marking scheme and help you to judge the appropriateness of your child's answers. Different children will have different ways of wording the correct answer. Focus on the content of an answer, judging whether your child 'had the right idea'.

Insert the mark gained for each answer in the box adjoining the question on the outside of each page of the Reading Test. Make sure the mark you record is equal to or less than the mark(s) available for that question.

'Rescuing Gloria' Pages 3–7

Award one mark for each correct choice.

1	window	1 mark
2	cows and pigs	1 mark
3	get caught by someone old	1 mark
4	wanted her to notice him	1 mark
5	Land Rover	1 mark
6	friendly	1 mark
7	amazed	1 mark
8	he was losing his land	1 mark

Note to Parent

If your child has made no mark, or has circled two or more responses, no score is given. If he or she has underlined, ticked or indicated his or her choice in another way, then score the responses as indicated above.

9 The correct order is as follows:

4 Leo stops by a Land Rover.
7 Leo meets the old man who owns Gloria.
3 Leo hears a new baby scream worse than Alice.
1 Leo moves to a new home.
6 Harjinder rescues Leo.
2 Leo spots the girl watering plants.
5 A goat tugs Leo's jacket.

Award one mark for getting the start and end points correct (that is, getting 2 and 7 in the right place).

Award two marks for correctly ordering all stages. *2 marks*

10 Award one mark for simplistic answers, e.g.

He is fed-up and unhappy.

Award two marks for answers which are more developed, e.g.

It shows he is embarassed and lacking confidence in his ability to make friends. *2 marks*

11 Award one mark for simplistic answers, e.g.

He has good ideas.

Award two marks for more developed answers, e.g.

He has an inventive mind to be able to think up ingenious solutions to difficult problems.

He is rather impetuous. He says things on the spur of the moment. *2 marks*

12 Award one mark for simplistic answers, e.g.

> *She is kind and has a good idea.*

Award two marks for more developed answers, e.g.

> *She is thoughtful and inventive. She knows how to get animals to do things.*   *2 marks*

13 Accept any answer which indicates that he has so far failed to get to know any people.   *1 mark*

14 Award one mark for answers such as:

> *He was being kind to her.*

Award another mark if appropriate evidence is also provided, e.g.

> *Leo talking to the goat/scratching her ears*
>
> *Gloria turning towards Leo, snuffling her nose into his hand*
>
> *Leo pulling gently at one of her ears.*   *2 marks*

15 Award one mark for any answer which refers to
living in a flat.

Award two marks for answers which give extra information, e.g.

> *the old garden not being part of his house*
>
> *not having asked his parents.*   *2 marks*

16 Award one mark for simple answers, e.g.

> *Yes, because he hasn't been able to make friends with any young people.*
>
> *No, because he talks to Gloria's owner.*

Award two marks for more elaborate answers which show evidence of more thoughtful reading, e.g.

> *Yes, because it is difficult being a young person in a new area.*
>
> *No, because he is feeling very unhappy to begin with. His feelings are likely to settle.*
>
> *No, people sometimes exagerate when they are in strange situations.*
>
> *No, when he actually meets an old person he is able to get on with him.*   *2 marks*

17 Award one mark if three words from the following list are given. Award a second mark if four or five appropriate words are given:

> *glared   hated   stamped   angrily   scowled   worse.*   *2 marks*

18 Award one mark if three words from this list are given:

> *forest   crowded   spreading   thick   green   leaves*
>
> *climbed   hung   drooped   hidden.*   *1 mark*

19 Award one mark if the explanation shows understanding that the building of a motorway has led to the old man leaving his home, meaning that there is nowhere for Gloria to live.   *1 mark*

20 Award one mark for

> *harshly.*   *1 mark*

21 Accept either YES or NO, but do not give a score for either response.

Score the reasons given as follows:

Award one mark for simplistic reasons, e.g.

> *It was good/it was boring.*

Award two marks for a slightly more elaborate answer, possibly involving references to the texts or personal preferences, e.g.

> *I liked/did not like the way it was written.*
>
> *I liked it when the goat grabbed Leo.*

Award three marks for a well justified answer revealing close reference to the text, e.g.

> *I thought it was slow moving and more should have happened.*
>
> *I thought the story told me about people's feelings.*
>
> *I felt sorry for Leo/Gloria and hoped things would get better for him/her.*
>
> *I thought that a lot had happened already.*
>
> *I wanted to know what would happen to Gloria.*
>
> *I thought the characters and situations were like real life.*   *3 marks*

22 Award one mark to answers which make an acceptable prediction about the rest of the story and two marks to those that accompany the prediction with a sensible explanation.

Acceptable predictions include:

> *making friends*
>
> *giving Gloria a good home/looking after her*
>
> *changing attitude to old people.*

Do not accept answers which refer only to getting the goat to her new home as these relate only to the next episode.   *2 marks*

Total 32 marks

'GOOD NEIGHBOURS' *Page 8*

1 Award one mark (up to three) for any of the following:

(i) *looking after gardens*		*1 mark*
(ii) *run errands*		*1 mark*
(iii) *housework.*		*1 mark*

2 Award one mark for answers which refer to cleaning up the litter/mess.   *1 mark*

3 Award one mark for simple answers, e.g.

> *She thinks it's a good idea.*

Award two marks for expanded ideas, e.g.

> *She thinks it's good for the old people to feel cared for and for the children to be understanding.*

Note: Other reasons from the article are valid.   *2 marks*

4   Award one mark for any quotation from the text which reveals the positive opinions. Positive answers include:

> *... their lives being made brighter ...*

> *... improving relationships ...*

> *Old and young have fun together.*

> *... the splendid efforts of these Yorkshire youngsters ...*

Check that the response is an actual quotation from the text.   *1 mark*

LETTERS *Pages 8–9*

5   Award one mark if **BOTH** parts of the question are answered correctly:

> *'I hope the excellent links between the generations will continue when the children go to High School' – Jane*

> *'Isn't school about learning about Maths, Science and English, rather than visiting the elderly?' – Martin*   *1 mark*

6a   Award one mark for answers which refer to:

> *hair and mud.*   *1 mark*

  b Award one mark for answers which make reference to all or any of the following:

> *hair   allergies   asthma.*   *1 mark*

7a   Award one mark for the police.   *1 mark*

  b Award one mark for any or all of these words:

> *pleasure respecting valuing friends good to read*

> *helping others unselfish praise and encouragement.*   *1 mark*

8   Award one mark for answers which contain elements of a personal response, although justification from the text may be weak, e.g.

> *'I agree with Jane – it's a good scheme.'*

Award two marks for answers revealing a grasp of the points and a personal response justified from the text, e.g.

> *'I agree with the article. People of different ages should get on with each other. Young and old are gaining. The old are helped and get company, the young are learning from the old.'*

Do not accept answers which do not express a personal view or fail to refer intelligently to the text, e.g.

> *'Jane's because she's right.'*   *2 marks*

Total 14 marks

'Old Johnny Armstrong' *Pages 10–11*

1   Award one mark for answers which refer to any of the following:

    his physical condition

    the shape of his body

    wondering what life has been about.   *1 mark*

2   Award one mark for answers which refer to any of the following:

    street lights   *trams*

    traffic   *blocks of flats*

    Benwell once being a village.   *1 mark*

3   Award one mark for any answer which conveys a sense of being a prisoner and/or being alone/isolated.   *1 mark*

4   Award one mark for simple, superficial responses, e.g.

    He likes to go there.

    Award two marks for answers which show an understanding of any one of the following:

    he went there as a child

    could run wild

    his body was straight

    good times and memories

    the trees and wind are the same as when he was a child.   *2 marks*

5   This is very much about personal insights and feelings.

    Award one mark for simple, superficial responses, e.g.

    'I feel sorry for him.'

    Award two marks for more developed responses, e.g.

    'It is sad that he is crippled and has few visitors. I am glad that he can manage to get to the park and remember his childhood.'   *2 marks*

6   Allow one mark for answers along the following lines:

    The sounds give a sense of the wind and the space. They make you feel the freedom of his childhood.   *1 mark*

                                           Total 8 marks

BOOKSHELF *Page 11*

1   Award one mark for each correct answer.

    (ii) His sister Alice: *Woof*

    (iii) The girl watering plants: *The Houseplant Survival Manual*

    (iv) The old man: *Land Rover 90/110 and Defender Owner's Workshop Manual*

    (v) Leo: *The New Goat Handbook*   *4 marks*

2   Give two marks for any answer which refers to:

   (i) books that help you to do things

   (ii) books that tell us stories.

   There may be alternative answers which refer to:

   (i) books for children

   (ii) books for adults

   Give one mark for such an answer.

2 marks
Total 6 marks

Improving your child's reading at KS2

- Do talk with your child about what he or she is reading and the way words are used.

- Talk, also, about what YOU are reading.

- Share a range of texts: stories, poems and non-fiction (including items from newspapers and magazines).

- Emphasise reading for different purposes – for example, enjoyment, information, instructions, reference.

- Understanding can be improved by encouraging your child to underline and label important words or sections when appropriate.

- Encourage your child to list the main points that are important in a text.

- Let your child devise his or her own questions for a text or section of a text.

- Encourage your child to use a variety of visual representation (e.g. drawings, maps, diagrams) to show characters, setting or information from texts.

- Read together: improve prediction skills by halting the reading at crucial moments so that your child can speculate on what might happen next, using cues from the text.

- Treat reading as a pleasure.

Information for the parent
Writing at KS2: AT3

Effective teaching and learning at KS2 will have taken place when planned from the Programmes of Study for English and implemented in classrooms where talk, reading and writing are integrated. A wide range of evidence about your child as a writer is available to his or her teacher; no test can identify and give a level to the full range of *any* writer's abilities.

The KS2 writing test focuses on several elements from the Programmes of Study. It is designed to gather evidence about a child's ability to:

- plan, draft, revise, proofread when writing;
- present clearly;
- construct and convey meaning in written language, matching style to audience and purpose;
- control more complex story forms – attending to structure, detail, setting, character and outcome;
- make meaning clear to the reader and engage the reader's interest;
- use literary stylistic features and be adventurous with vocabulary choices;
- use a wide range of sentence connectives;
- attend to punctuation which demarcates sentences (capital letters, full stops, question marks, exclamation marks);
- set out and punctuate direct speech;
- use commas and paragraphs;
- use written Standard English (except where non-standard or spoken forms are appropriate);
- use pronouns so that things or persons referred to are easily identified;
- use verb tenses in order that shifts in time are consistently and accurately managed;
- ensure agreement between subject and verb within a sentence.

Assessing your child's answer

A full picture of any writer's achievements can only be built up over a period of time in a range of situations. Your child's teacher will have a much fuller view from what has been written during Key Stage 2 than any one-hour test can possibly give. His or her professional skills will provide insight which a parent will be unlikely to match.

The writing test attempts to identify the young writer's achievements in three broad categories:

- Purpose and Organisation

- Grammar

- Style

Few children develop uniformly across these categories.

In marking your child's work, you will be identifying your child's positive achievements as a writer and making judgements about relative strengths and weaknesses in each category. Use the Writing Assessment Criteria table on pages 39–41 to help you to determine your child's score. You will see that your child doesn't need to match all the criteria shown at each level to gain that level. Read the examples of how Cathy's, Sarbjit's and Emily's writing was marked on pages 31–38.

Fill in the box on page 18 with your child's marks.

Example achievements at AT3 (writing)

Before assessing your child's writing use the Writing Assessment Criteria table (pages 39–41) to identify levels of achievement in writing by three Year 6 pupils, Cathy, Sarbjit and Emily. Start by reading 'Making Friends' by Cathy.

MAKING FRIENDS
written by Cathy Summers
(first draft, with Cathy's own spelling and punctuation)

My name is Cathy Summers. I used to live in Walsall but when I was ten my mum and dad decided to move to Wales because life would be better in the countryside. They put our house up for sale. I was very upset and so were my friends. The day came to move, it was very sad. I was quietly crying and so were my friends. When the family got to Wales we unpacked and I just sat in my new bedroom and cried. My mum came up and tried to comfort me but it didn't work because of the loneliness. About three weeks passed and I never went out not even to school because it was the summer holidays. By now I was fed up. I didn't want to spend my summer hols like this. There was some shops up the road so I decided to ask my Mum for some money so I could go to the shops to buy some sweets. She said 'yes' so off I went. There were some girls and a boy about my age sitting on a wall. They looked bored but friendly. I walked passed to make myself noticed.

3/4 of first page

I looked up for a second and some of them smiled so I smiled back. On my way back from the shops I walked passed the group that were still on the wall. One of them, a thin blonde girl said Hia. What's your name? "Mine is Cathy, what's yours?" I asked. "My name's Adelle, this is Rhiannon, this is Cheryl and this is Philip. You are new here aren't you?" said Adele smiling.

End of first page

I was really happy. I'd made some friends and couldn't wait to tell my Mum. I asked "Any one want a sweet?" "please" they all said together. We all started laughing and I handed the sweets out. Afterwards I hardly had any left but it didn't matter, they were my new friends.

PURPOSE AND ORGANISATION

Refer to the table for Purpose and Organisation on page 39. Begin at Level 3. How does Cathy's story fulfil the criteria?

- There is some description of feelings and motives.
  'I was very upset and so were my friends.'
  '... it was very sad. I was quietly crying ...'
  '... I was really happy ...'
  'I walked passed to make myself noticed.'

- There is detail adding interest.
  '... some of them smiled so I smiled back.'

- Some sensible relation exists between events.
  Events that are connected. Cathy has selected things that are pertinent to her story.

- There is a simple ending relating to the topic.
  'Afterwards I hardly had any left but it didn't matter, they were my new friends.'

Three or more criteria at Level 3 are clearly demonstrated. Cathy is achieving at Level 3. What evidence is there of achievement at Level 4? Look at the criteria for this level. Does Cathy's story meet three or more of these?

- There is a logical relationship between the events of Cathy's story. The relocation leads to loneliness, the trip to the shops to a meeting with new friends, the new friends lead to happiness. There is some paragraphing.

- There is some characterisation and there is significant interaction – between Cathy and her old friends, Cathy and her mother and Cathy and her new friends.

- Description is used to develop characterisation.
  Her mother's actions convey kindness.
  'They looked bored but friendly.'
  The laughter conveys happiness.

- Given the limitations of time, Cathy has paced her story. It is detailed, there is a clear beginning, middle and end.

- Awareness of the reader is shown through comments about events and characters.
  '... life would be better in the countryside ...'
  '... they were my new friends.'
  '... because it was the summer holidays.'

Cathy has clearly demonstrated achievement against three or more criteria at Level 4. Is there evidence of any achievements at Level 5?

- There is evidence of competence in using story conventions but *not* of flexibility.

- The central plot is convincing.

- Although dialogue, action and description are used, these are not developed.

- Indications of thoughts and feelings are limited – there is no development of viewpoint or narrative.

- Paragraphing is not consistent.

Although this story shows some evidence of achievement at Level 5 it is insufficient for that level to be given. It does meet sufficient criteria at Level 4 (Purpose and Organisation), therefore award 8 marks.

GRAMMAR

Next refer to the table for Grammar on page 40 and see how Cathy's story meets the criteria. Begin at Level 3.

- At least half of the sentences on the first page are correctly punctuated with capital letters and full stops or question marks. Cathy has clearly achieved Level 3.

Now compare the grammar of her story with the criteria for Level 4.

- At least 3/4 of the sentences are correctly punctuated using capital letters followed by full stops, question marks or exclamation marks.

- Commas are used to separate items on a list.
  '... this is Rosylyn, this is Cheryl, this is Philip.'

- Speech punctuation is generally accurate.

- The use of pronouns is inconsistent but pronouns are used.

Cathy has clearly demonstrated achievement against two or more criteria at Level 4. Is there evidence of any achievements at Level 5?

- There are more than two lapses in punctuation.
  'please' (capital letter missing)
  Hia. What's your name (speech marks and question mark missing)

- Tenses and pronouns used consistently.

Cathy does not meet sufficient criteria for Level 5 (Grammar). She has met sufficient criteria for Level 4, therefore award 4 marks.

STYLE

Now refer to the table for Style on page 41 and identify Cathy's achievements, beginning at Level 3.

- There is use of connectives.
  'because', 'when', 'but', 'by', 'now'

- There are simple noun phrases.
  'my new bedroom', 'a blond girl'

One or more criteria for style are met: Level 3 is achieved for Style. Now identify achievements for Level 4.

- There is a preponderance of written language structures. Cathy informs us of her name and situation, avoids repetition and summarises when necessary. She uses the literary convention of resolution at the end of her story.

- Subordinating connectives are used.
  'By now...', 'because of...'

- There is use of expansion before or after the subject noun.
  '... *about my age, sitting on a wall*'
  '... *not even to school*'

Two or more criteria at Level 4 are met. Are there achievements at Level 5?

- The story is in written in Standard English and she uses dialect (slang 'Hia') when appropriate.

- She does not differentiate speech from writing using complex sentence structures.

- Vocabulary is not particularly varied and interesting.

Cathy does not meet two or more criteria Level 5 (Style). Her story does meet sufficient criteria for Level 4 (Style) so 4 marks are awarded and Cathy's writing test score looks like this:

	Cathy's Writing Test Score
Purpose and Organisation	8
Grammar	4
Style	4
WRITING TEST TOTAL	16

Now consider a second story, 'Future Life' by Sarbjit.

FUTURE LIFE
by Sarbjit Kapoor
(first draft, with Sarbjit's own spelling and punctuation)

The year is 2050 A.D.
The date 20/11/50
The place Oldham, Lands End (due to raised sea-level due to global warming), England.

My Grandad, Sarbjit Kapoor, had first told me about his Ford XR3 convertible when I was ten in 2044. It had been his first car, he'd bought it in 2002 A.D. He told me how he'd saved and saved to buy it after he passed his driving test. The car was already ten years old then. 'The best car in the universe' he claimed. 'Is there such a thing,' I'd asked 'I'd settle for the worst car in the world. I'd settle for any car at all!' 'Well when you are sixteen I'll take you out for a drive, but don't tell your Mum,' he whispered.

The sun rose early – a green dawn like flourescent gas. The atmosphere had never been clear since the war between Japan and the U.S.A.
'I've managed to get some petrol my old friend Darren had.'
'Great Grandad, the roboid cars now are all electric or gas.'
'I'll drive us out to the old motorway across the moors – the M62, I know a secret way onto a smooth bit.' 'We'll after look out for Police Capsules.'

It was my sixteenth birthday – the time had come for my first drive in A MOTORCAR! My name is Zeeko Kapoor. I live in an underground house near Oldham, overlooking the sea. 9/10th of the world is now ocean because of global warming. I live with my family and my Grandad.

My heart was beating like a hammer with excitement. Would he let me have a drive, I wondered. I'd never been in a real car before.

Grandad turned the ignition key. The engine coughed and spluttered, the car jumped forward. Soon we were doing fifty miles an hour, the wind rushing through my hair, my eyes were stung by it.

It was really great, cars now were all Roboids, very safe but VERY boring. The old car was a bit rattly even though Grandad had looked after it carefully.

33

'FASTER' I shouted, we were now doing 90 m.p.h. Suddenly he slammed the brakes on.
'Look out,' I screamed.
After that everything went black.
I awoke to find my parents gathered around my bed.
'How's Grandad?' I asked.
'He's O.K.' said Dad.
'What happened?'
'You hit a sheep, Grandad swerved and you left the motoway.'
'It's all my fault, I wanted him to go faster.'
'Don't worry son, Grandad hasn't enjoyed himself so much since he won the British Grand Prix in 2010 A.D.' laughed Dad.

Later that day Granded was moved into the same ward.
'I've got some great news,' he told me, 'We're being sent to the space hospital to recover! They say the lack of gravity gets you better quicker.'
'That was a great drive, you can see why cars are banned.'
'Yes, but it's a pity the car was smashed up.' It had been a great day.

PURPOSE AND ORGANISATION

Refer to the table for Purpose and Organisation on page 39 to consider whether Sarbjit's story meets the criteria for Level 4.

- The events do relate. There is paragraphing.

- Characters are developed, they do interact.
  'It was my sixteenth birthday.'

- Development within the action conveys character.
  'The best car in the universe' he claimed.
  'Is there such a thing,' I'd asked.

- The story is paced and detailed, with a beginning, middle and end.

- Comments show awareness of the reader.
  'I live with my family and my Grandad ...'

Three or more criteria are clearly demonstrated: Level 4 is achieved. Is there achievement at Level 5 – does Sarbjit meet three or more of these criteria?

- Use of story conventions is competent and flexible.
  He opens the main action half way through the circumstances ('My Grandad, Sarbjit Kapoor, had first ...')
  There is use of snatches of dialogue.
  'The best car in the world ...'
  '... don't tell your Mum,' he whispered.
  There is synopsis.
  'It had been his first car, he'd bought it in 2002 A.D.'

- The plot and ending are convincing.

- The point of view and narrative voice are developed.
  'Would he let me have a drive, I wondered?'
  'It was really great, cars now were all Roboids, very safe but VERY boring.'
  'It had been a great day.'

- Paragraphs do consistently mark major episodes.

Certainly three or more criteria for Purpose and Organisation are met. Sarbjit's story is definitely Level 5. Is there evidence of achievements at Level 6?

- Within the limits of this task we see themes (technological change, environmental change) developed.

- There are a number of linked episodes.

- There is some reflection on characters and actions, the story moves backwards and forwards in time, suspense or surprise is less marked.

- Paragraphing ensures coherent organisation.

- Spoken dialogue is clearly laid out.

Three or more criteria for Level 6 (Purpose and Organisation) are met. Award 12 marks.

GRAMMAR

Now refer to the table for Grammar on page 40. Compare Sarbjit's criteria with the criteria for Level 3. The criteria are met. The same is true of Levels 4 and 5. Both criteria at Level 6 are met. Therefore award 6 marks.

STYLE

Now refer to the table for Style on page 41 and identify Sarbjit's achievements, beginning at Level 4.

- Written language structures are used.

- Subordinating connectives are used.
  'Suddenly,' 'After that...'

- Expansion is used before or after subject nouns.
  'the worst car in the world.'
  'the old motorway across the moors.'

Two or more criteria for Level 4 (Style) are met. Now compare the story to the criteria for Level 5.

- There is no choice of dialect in the story. Sarbjit has chosen to use Standard English throughout, therefore that criteria is met.

- Speech and writing are differentiated. Sarbjit uses the passive voice.
  'The sun rose early –' The subject of the sentence (the sun) is the 'goal' of the action.
  'My eyes were stung by it.' The subject of the phrase (my eyes) is the goal of the action.

He also avoids repetition, referring backwards and forwards to subject matter.

- Varied and interesting vocabulary are recognised.
  'a green dawn like flourescent gas.'
  'My heart was beating like a hammer'

Sarbjit has met two or more criteria for Level 5 (Style).

It is now worth comparing the story with the criteria for Level 6.

- Noun phrases are expanded and elaborated; there is use of simile.
  'overlooking the sea.'
  'the wind rushing through my hair...'
  'a green dawn like flourescent gas'
  'like a hammer with excitement'

- There is a varied choice of verbs.
  'claimed', 'asked', 'whispered'

- The order of words and phrases within sentences is chosen to develop themes and sustain interest.
  'a green dawn like flourescent gas.'
  'The time had come for my first drive in A MOTOR CAR!'

- Deliberate patterning for emphasis and rhythm appears in Sarbjit's story.

  'The best car in the universe' he claimed. 'Is there such a thing,' I asked 'I'd settle for the worst car in the world. I'd settle for any car at all!'

- Sarbjit has not chosen to use dialect for characterisation.

Sarbjit meets three or more criteria at Level 6. Six marks should be awarded and his Writing Test Score looks like this:

	Sarbjit's Writing Test Score
Purpose and Organisation	12
Grammar	6
Style	6
WRITING TEST TOTAL	24

When setting a level for your child's story, remember that only a number of the criteria need to be met for that level to be awarded as stated in the Writing Assessment Criteria table on pages 39–41.

Given the limitations of this test do be positive in your review of the evidence. Sarbjit's story is particularly full of evidence: quite small examples are sufficient for the criteria to be met.

Now consider a piece of descriptive writing, 'My Grandad Drever' by Emily.

MY GRANDAD DREVER
by Emily Drever
(first draft, with Emily's own spelling and punctuation)

My Grandad Drever lives on his own in a bungalow near Church Lawton. He has lived there since he retired. He used to have his own business as a plumber.

He is a very kind man and laughs a lot. He is 69 years old and has been on his own since my Nan died in 1992. He loves his garden. It is always very tidy and full of flowers. He grows beautiful roses.

Every Sunday Grandad Drever visits us for his tea. He always brings me a present, sometimes chocolate or sweets, sometimes something interesting he has bought at a car-boot. Last week he got me a coral necklace. It is nice of him to get me things but I don't always like them. I pretend I do!

He likes car-boot sales. He buys old brass and shines it up and sells it. He also makes bird houses and bird tables and sells them.

3/4 of first page

I think he misses my Nan a lot. He likes to show me photographs of them when they were young.

He is a fit man. He walks his dog, Megan, every day down by the canal. He is tall and has white hair. He eyes are blue and his skin is very tanned.

End of first page

There are little lines on his face. He does not watch much television, except travel programmes. He likes wildlife and different parts of the world. My Grandad is a good friend to me, I love him very much.

PURPOSE AND ORGANISATION

Refer to the table for Purpose and Organisation on page 39. Elements of Level 4 are clearly shown.

* There is some logic to the structure and paragraphs are used. Character is developed by description as is setting.
  'full of flowers'
  'He is a very kind man and laughs a lot.'

* Comments develop this description.
  '... I don't always like them.'
  '... he misses my Nan a lot.'

* The description is paced and detailed and Emily shows awareness of the reader through comments.
  '... I don't always like them.'
  'My Grandad is a good friend to me... '

Three or more criteria for Level 4 are clearly demonstrated. It's now necessary to check for achievements at Level 5; does the writer meet three or more of these?

* Description is developed.
  '... he grows beautiful roses.'
  '... he is tall and has white hair. His eyes are blue and his skin is very tanned. There are little lines on his face.'

* Narrative voice is also developed.
  '... I pretend I do!'
  'I think he misses my Nan a lot.'

* Paragraph divisions consistently mark major episodes of the writing.

Emily has met three criteria at Level 5. A review of criteria for Level 6 shows that she fails to meet sufficient criteria, therefore she is awarded ten marks.

GRAMMAR

Now refer to the table for Grammar on page 40. This shows that Emily has achieved two criteria for Level 5.

At Level 6 we find that she uses punctuation, tenses and pronouns effectively throughout.

Has she decided to vary sentence length for clarity and change of pace to help the reader? The difficulty of judging this underlines the limitations of National Curriculum testing – looking, as it does, at limited evidence.

Experience of the marking in 1995 suggests that Emily has *not* achieved both criteria for Level 6. Award five marks only.

Now consider Emily's story against the criteria for Style on page 41.

- At Level 4 written language structures are used, repetition is avoided and there is summary.
  '... he always brings me something interesting.'

- Subordinating connectives give meaning.
  '... but I don't always like them.'
  'He also makes bird houses... '

Emily gains Level 4 for Style. Does she meet Level 5? Standard English is quite appropriately used, as are written language constructions. Vocabulary is generally varied and interesting. This is sufficient for Level 5.

Next check the writing against Level 6 for Style.

- Noun phrases are expanded and elaborated.
  'He is a very kind man and laughs a lot.'
  'He likes to show me photographs of them when they were young.'

- There is little variation in verbs or abverbs. 'Enjoyed', 'appreciate', 'loves', would make effective alternatives to the much-used 'like'. 'Very' is also over-used.

- There is some attempt to vary the order of phrases. 'Last week...' and 'Every Sunday...' make a change from beginning sentences 'He... ' or 'My Grandad... '.

Emily is able to pattern for emphasis and rhythm.
'... sometimes chocolate or sweets, sometimes something interesting... '
'I pretend I do! I love him very much.'

She has met three or more criteria for Style. Award six marks.

	Emily's Writing Test Score
Purpose and Organisation	10
Grammar	5
Style	6
WRITING TEST TOTAL	21

Writing assessment criteria

1	PURPOSE AND ORGANISATION	Maximum 12 marks

LEVEL 3	*As a whole the writing shows:* • some detail in the description of setting or characters' feelings or motives • details adding interest or humour or suspense • some sensible relation between events or ideas (i.e. selected highlights from chronological sequence, not every happening) • a simple ending relating to topic. **Award 6 marks if two or more criteria (●) are met.**
LEVEL 4	• ideas or events in the writing relate to each other logically and with some paragraphing • story 'characters' developed for the purpose of the story, some significant interaction between them or personality of central figure developed • characterisation developed within the writing (e.g. by use of direct or reported speech or by description) • length of writing well judged with respect to pacing and detail; beginning, middle and end suitably distinguished • comments on characters or events show awareness of reader (these may be quite brief). **Award 8 marks if three or more criteria (●) are met.**
LEVEL 5	• competent and flexible use of story or descriptive conventions, e.g. ability to experiment with story opening – starting in the middle of circumstances, or with snatches of dialogue, or with narrator's synopsis • convincing central plot or character and ending or conclusion • ability to interweave elements of dialogue, action, description where appropriate • development of point of view and 'narrative voice' (e.g. asides to reader, comments on action, indication of character's thoughts and/or feelings) • paragraph divisions mark major episodes of story (e.g. beginning, start of action and/or final resolution), different aspects of central character described. **Award 10 marks if three or more criteria (●) are met.**
LEVEL 6	• development of theme (e.g. loneliness, friendship) or personality (e.g. humour, kindness) as well as plot (the happenings of the story) or, in a descriptive piece, the attitudes or values of the person • contains a number of linked episodes or sections • relationship/conflict between characters • reflections on characters and actions and, if appropriate, non-linear time line, management of suspense or surprise • use of paragraphs to ensure coherent organisation • any spoken dialogue is clearly laid out. **Award 12 marks if three or more criteria (●) are met.**

2	GRAMMAR	Maximum 6 marks

LEVEL 3

Assess on the first full page:

- at least half the sentences are correctly punctuated using capital letters and full stops or question marks.

Award 3 marks if this criteria (•) is met.

LEVEL 4

Assess on first full page:

- at least three-quarters of the sentences are correctly punctuated using capital letters followed by full stops, question marks or exclamation marks
- developing use of comma to separate phrases or clauses in sequence, items on list
- speech punctuation generally accurate
- consistent use of tenses and pronouns.

Award 4 marks if two or more criteria (•) are met.

LEVEL 5

Assess on first full page:

- no more than two lapses in punctuation of sentences, or in direct speech
- consistent and appropriate use of tenses and pronouns.
- accurate punctuation of speech

Award 5 marks if two or more criteria (•) are met.

LEVEL 6

Assess on complete text:

- sustained accurate use of punctuation (see above), tenses, pronouns
- evidence of decisions to vary sentence length for clarity and change of narrative pace to help the reader.

Award 6 marks if both criteria (•) are met.

40

3	STYLE	Maximum 6 marks

LEVEL 3	**Assess on the writing as a whole:** • evidence of beginning to shape writing by use of a wider range of connectives (e.g. *'but'*, *'when'*, *'so'*, *'because'*, etc.) to indicate relation between ideas (e.g. *'contrast'*, *'connection in time'*, *'explanation'*) **Award 3 marks**
LEVEL 4	• greater use of written language structures, e.g. avoids repetition • use of subordinating connectives to give meaning (e.g. *'as if'*, *'instead'*, *'so that'*, *'because of'*, *'although'*) • beginning of use of expansion before or after the subject noun for description and comment (e.g. *'battered Land Rover'*, *'a goat with bad breath'*). **Award 4 marks if two or more criteria (•) are met.**
LEVEL 5	• appropriate choice between Standard English, dialect and colloquialism • differentiation of speech from writing: e.g. clear use of written language constructions, such as passive voice, to alter focus of attention (e.g. *'I was surrounded by friends'*) e.g. use of constructions to avoid repetition, such as grouping of several subjects before a main verb, referring back/forward to subject matter, using *'that'*, *'these'*, *'it'* • greater use of varied and interesting vocabulary. **Award 5 marks if two or more criteria (•) are met.**
LEVEL 6	• expansion and elaboration of noun phrases to enhance description of characters and feelings – similes or metaphors may be used • varied choice of verbs (e.g. *'screamed'*, *'begged'*), and adverbs (e.g. *'two reasonably well behaved children'*) gives shades of meaning • within sentences, order of words and phrases chosen to develop themes of story and sustain reader interest • deliberate patterning for emphasis and rhythm (e.g. *'Thunder sounded, lightning flashed and hard rain began to pour'*) • use of dialect, slang or colloquialism if needed, for characterisation. **Award 6 marks if three or more criteria (•) are met.**

Improving your child's writing at KS2

- Use paragraphs: ideas which go together in separate sections, starting on a new line.
- Use some spoken dialogue, set down correctly using speech marks and a new line for each person speaking.
- Punctuate correctly.
- Use tenses and pronouns correctly.
- Use varied, interesting vocabulary.
- Use descriptive language to convey settings, characters and feelings.
- Use metaphors and similes when appropriate.

PLAN, DRAFT AND IMPROVE

- **plan** – note and develop initial ideas;
- **draft** – develop ideas from the plan into structured written text;
- **revise** – alter and improve the draft;
- **proofread** – check the draft for spelling and punctuation errors, ommissions or repetitions;
- **present** – prepare a neat, correct and clear final copy.

CAPITAL LETTERS

Remind your child of the purpose of capital letters.

1   As the first letter of a sentence
    He went on walking.

2   For the personal pronoun 'I'
    I did not hurt her.

3   At the beginning of a new piece of direct speech
    Leo shouted, *"Come on, you crazy goat."*

4   For the first letter of a proper noun
    People's names: *Gillian Cross*
    Places: *High Street, Coventry, England*
    Titles of books, plays, films, TV programmes:
        Rescuing Gloria, Horizon

    Days of the week: *Wednesday*
    Brand names: *Land Rover*
    Months of the year: *August*
    Planets and stars: *Venus*

5   For the first letter of titles of people and organisations
    The Prince of Wales; Royal Society for the Protection of Birds

6   For the initials in the names of people and organisations
    Edward G. Robinson; Liverpool F.C.

7   For initials used in abbreviations
    BBC, RSPCA

FULL STOPS, QUESTIONS MARKS AND EXCLAMATION MARKS

Normal sentences must end with one of these three marks:

     .   ?   !
full stop   question mark   exclamation mark

Statements normally end with a **full stop**.
There was a goat in the back.

42

A **question** normally ends with a **question mark**.
What can I do?

Exclamation marks are used to mark an **exclamation**, or **forceful statement**.
But that's six weeks!

COMMAS

Commas help a reader pass over the page of print. They make sentences easier to read and understand. They are used to:

1   Separate the items in a list
    At Christmas they bought me a Christmas tree, decorations, mince pies, and a present.

2   Separate the clauses in a sentence
    Gloria the goat turned towards him, snuffling her nose into his hand as he got close.

3   Mark off phrases that are separate from the main part of the sentence.
    It was the holidays, after all, and people from the school must be hanging around somewhere.

WRITING DOWN DIRECT SPEECH

1   Every piece of speech is enclosed between double or single inverted commas. In books single inverted commas are normally used. In school your child may have been taught to use double inverted commas.

2   Every new piece of speech must begin with a capital letter, even if it is not the first word in the sentence.

3   Each piece of speech must end with a full stop or an exclamation mark or a question mark before the concluding inverted commas...

4   ... unless the sentence is going to continue, when it ends with a comma. This also comes before the concluding inverted commas.

5   For each new speaker you start a new line and indent.

    'I wasn't hurting her,' Leo said quickly. 'Only talking to her.'
    'I can tell that, boy. She likes you.' The old man took a chunk of cabbage out of his pocket. 'Give her this.'
    Rather nervously, Leo took the cabbage and held it out. Gloria lunged forward to take a bite.
    'That's it, girl,' the old man said. His voice crackled strangely. 'You have some fun while you can. You've only got another ten minutes or so.'
    Leo looked at Gloria as she chewed. 'Why only ten minutes? What's going to happen then?'

SIMILES AND METAPHORS

A similie is used when something is said to be like something else:
'He humps like a question-mark' – the shape of his body is compared to a question mark.
'A Council Block that rears like a rock' – the block of flats is compared to a rock.

A metaphor is when something is said to have become something else.
'... seas of swirled traffic' – the traffic has become a sea.
'... his cell on the seventeenth floor' – his room has become a cell.

Notes

Use this space to make notes about the achievements you have identified in your child's piece of writing.

Spelling and Handwriting Test answers

Information for the parent
Spelling and Handwriting at KS2: part of AT3

During the course of Key Stage 2 children have been enabled to develop their individual ability in recognising, knowing and applying:

- single syllable words which follow common patterns
  cold, sold, gold

- regularly used multi-syllable words
  because, animal, together, planet

- common regular vowel patterns and letter strings
  slave, cave, grave; –ing, –ion, –ous

- word families and their relationships
  freeze, freezing, frozen; sleep, sleeping, slept

- more complex words
  crumble, crumbling, crumbled; accident, accidental

- words with related meaning which have related spellings, even though they sound different
  sign, signature; medical, medicine; manage, managerial

- alternative ways of writing the same sound
  caught, court; stare, stair; roar, floor; cell, sell

- the spelling of words with inflectional endings
  hard, harder, hardest

- the meaning, use and spelling of common prefixes and suffixes
  –er, –ing, –ly, –less, –ed, –ion

- the use of the apostrophe to spell shortened forms of words
  I am, I'm; they will, they'll, she has, she's

- complex polysyllabic words that conform to regular patterns
  marvellous, generous, humorous, dangerous, enormous

- long and complex words broken into more manageable units
  dec/or/a/tion, acc/i/den/tal, con/quer/ing

- silent letters
  knew, climb, sign, doubt, listen, guard, who

- words with irregular visual patterns

- roots and origins of words

They have also developed their ability to produce handwriting in both joined and printed styles and which is fluent, legible, clear and attractive. They will have been taught to use different forms of handwriting for different purposes, e.g. print to label maps or diagrams; a clear, neat hand for finished presented work; a faster script for notes.

Note to Parent

Detatch this page so you can read this passage aloud while your child does the spelling test on pages 20–21.

Through Space in 'Eternity'

All around the Earth people **looked** on as the **time** rapidly **approached** for the launch of United Nations' deep space craft *Eternity*.

Their minds were **concentrating** on a billion virtual **reality** sets. The **power** of many lasers **illuminated** the launch site, cutting the African night; tension was mounting inside the command centre. After much **planning** the time had come to explore space in the remote control craft, seeking some **planet** on which human life could be established.

Why was this voyage taking place? By the year 2050 A.D. Earth had become even more crowded. The population multiplied and consumed at an ever-increasing rate. Human selfishness had destroyed **nature**, now humanity itself was threatened. It appeared that nothing **could** prevent an environmental disaster.

The **capacity** of the deep space craft was limited. From a million volunteers from all over the **world** one hundred were **carefully** chosen. Life on a new planet would be difficult. Tolerance, intelligence and confidence were particularly important qualities.

The journey they faced was long. Medical science knew how to **freeze** them, injections of **gold** would stop bones from **crumbling**, artificial **material** replaced blood.

Many dangers lay ahead. Barring **accidents**, the travellers would reach their destination in 2150 A.D., having **slept** for a **century!**

SPELLING TEST **Pages 20–21**

1	looked	*1 mark*
2	time	*1 mark*
3	approached	*1 mark*
4	concentrating	*1 mark*
5	reality	*1 mark*
6	power	*1 mark*
7	illuminated	*1 mark*
8	planning	*1 mark*
9	planet	*1 mark*
10	nature	*1 mark*
11	could	*1 mark*
12	capacity	*1 mark*
13	world	*1 mark*
14	carefully	*1 mark*
15	freeze	*1 mark*
16	gold	*1 mark*
17	crumbling	*1 mark*
18	material	*1 mark*
19	accidents	*1 mark*
20	century	*1 mark*

Total 20 marks

IMPROVING YOUR CHILD'S SPELLING AT KS2

PATTERNS

English spelling is not chaotic. Three-quarters of all words follow regular patterns. Encourage your child to be aware of patterns of letters used to spell particular sounds.

WORD FAMILIES

Encourage your child to look for word families.
author, authorise, authority, authorisation

In this family of four words *author* is spelled the same. *-ity, -ise, -isation* are spelled in the same way. Looking for families like this makes spelling easier.

A WAY TO LEARN SPELLINGS

1 **LOOK** at the correct spelling of the word and say it. It could help you to write it out five times.

2 **COVER** the word and **REMEMBER** it.

3 **WRITE** it from memory.

4 **CHECK** it with the original.

5 If it's wrong, repeat stages 1–4.

MAKING PLURALS

Plural means 'more than one'. Most words follow rules. For example:
1 Normally, just add **-s**.
  *book – book**s**.*

2 Words that end in **-s**, add **-es**.
  *glas**s** – glass**es***

3 Words that end in **-x** and **-z**, add **-es**.
  *fo**x** – fox**es***

4 Words that end in **-ch** and **-sh**, add **-es**.
  *bran**ch** – branch**es***

5 Words that end in **-f** or **-fe** change the ending to **-ve** and add **-s**.
  Exceptions: *belie**fs**, chie**fs**, dwar**fs**, grie**fs**, gul**fs**, proo**fs**, roo**fs***

6 Words that end in **-y**, if the letter before the **y** is a vowel just add **-s**.
  *da**y** – da**ys***

  If the letter before the **y** is a consonant change the **-y** to **-ies**.
  *bab**y** – bab**ies***

7 Words that end in **-o** usually just need an **-s**.
  *pian**o** – pian**os***
  Exceptions: *volcano**es**, hero**es**, tomato**es**, go**es**, potato**es***

8 Some words stay the same in the plural.
  aircraft, sheep, deer

9 Some words change in a different way.
  child – children
  mouse – mice
  woman – women

10 Some Latin and Greek words change in different ways.
crisis – crises
formula – formulae

ADDING -ING AND -ED

Verbs change according to the sentence they are in. Normally you just add **-ing** or **-ed**.

I walk to school. I <u>walked</u> to school yesterday and I am <u>walking</u> to school now.

Exceptions

The main exceptions are:

hop**e** – hop**ing**	cr**y** – cr**ied**
smok**e** – smok**ing**	tr**y** – tr**ied**
sto**p** – sto**pping**	sto**p** – sto**pped**
ru**n** – ru**nning**	

1   Word with one syllable, with a long vowel, ending in **-e**. Remove the **-e** and add **-ed** and **-ing**.
*dar**e**, dar**ed**, dar**ing***

2   Words with one syllable, with a short vowel, ending in a single consonant. Double the consonant and add **-ed** and **-ing**.
*beg, begg**ed**, begg**ing***

3   Words with more than one syllable, ending in a single consonant. If the last syllable is stressed, double the consonant.
*propel, propel**led**, propel**ling***

If the stress is not on the last syllable, just add **-ed** and **-ing**.
*sharpen, sharpen**ed**, sharpen**ing***

4   Words ending in **-l**. If there is only a single vowel before the **-l**, just add **-ed** and **-ing**.
*peel, peel**ed**, peel**ing***

5   Words ending in **-y**.
If the letter before the **-y** is a vowel, just add **-ed** and **-ing**.
*stay, stay**ed**, stay**ing***
Exceptions: *lay – laid, say – said, pay – paid*

If the letter before the **-y** is a consonant change the **-y** to an **-i** before adding **-ed**.
*fr**y**, fr**ied**, fr**ying***

ADDING -LY

Turn adjectives into adverbs by adding **-ly**.

*He is a slow driver. He drives slow**ly**.*

Usually you just add **-ly** to the adjective.

Exceptions

1   If the word ends in **-ll** just add **-y**.
*full – ful**ly***

2   If a word of two or more syllables ends in **-y** remove the **-y** and add **-ily**.
*happ**y** – happ**ily***

3   One-syllable words ending in **-y** are usually regular.
*sh**y** – shy**ly***
Exception: *day – daily*

4   If the words end in **-le** remove the **-e** and add **-y**.
*simp**le** – simp**ly***

READING BOOKS

Reading will not make everyone a perfect speller but it is difficult to be really good at spelling if you read nothing at all.

Assessing your child's handwriting

Compare your child's copy of the handwriting passage with these examples and decide which best matches his or her achievements.

Accurately formed letters, consistent in size, e.g.

> Who could say how successful their journey
> might be?
> Could this brave mission find a place for
> the human race somewhere deep in space?

2 marks

Handwriting *begins* to be joined and is legible, e.g.

> Who could say how successful their
> Journey might be?
> Could this brave mission find a
> place for the human race?

More fluent, joined and legible handwriting, e.g.

> Who could say how successful their journey might
> be? Could this brave mission find a place for
> the human race somewhere deep in space?

4 marks

Joined, clear, neat and fluent handwriting, e.g.

> Who could say how successful their journey might be?
> Could this brave mission find a place for the human
> race, somewhere deep in space?

Handwriting is consistently fluent and legible, clear and attractive, e.g.

> Who could say how successful their journey might be?
> Could this brave mission find a place for the human race
> somewhere deep in space?

6 marks

Total 6 marks

Improving your child's handwriting at KS2

Fluency and clarity may be improved by attending to these points:

- Sit in a relaxed, comfortable way, not too close to the table.
- Hold the pen so that there is control and comfort, avoiding tension and too tight a grip.
- Start all letters at the top except **d** and **e**.
- Make letters neither too large nor too small.
- All similar letters should be the same height.
- Strokes above (**b**, **d**, **f**, **h**, **k**, **l**, **t**) and below (**g**, **j**, **p**, **q**, **y**) should be clearly visible.

Finding your child's level for English

There are four stages to finding the overall English test level.

1 Note your child's Reading Test Total from page 11.

2 Note your child's Writing Test Total from page 18.

3 Use the table below to convert your child's Spelling Score from page 21 and your child's Handwriting Score from page 21 to find the Presentation Mark.

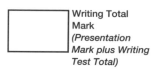

	Reading Test Total
	Writing Test Total
	Spelling Score
	Handwriting Score

Handwriting Score

Spelling Score	2	4	6
0	1	1	2
1–4	2	3	3
5–7	3	3	4
8–13	3	4	5
14–18	4	5	6
19–20	5	6	6

Read down from the column which contains your child's Handwriting Score and read across from the row giving your child's Spelling Score.

This Presentation Mark should be between 0 and 6.

Add the Presentation Mark and the Writing Test Total mark together. This gives the Writing Total Mark, between 0 and 30.

4 Now use the table below to find the English test level.

	Presentation Mark *(Spelling and Handwriting)*
	Writing Total Mark *(Presentation Mark plus Writing Test Total)*

Reading Test Total

Writing Total Mark (Presentation Mark plus Writing Test Total)	0–2	3–10	11–25	26–43	44–54	55–60
0–2	*	2	2	3	4	4
3–6	1	2	3	3	4	5
7–11	2	2	3	4	4	5
12–16	2	3	3	4	5	5
17–21	3	3	4	4	5	6
22–26	3	4	4	5	5	6
27–30	4	4	5	5	6	6

Read down from the column which contains your child's Reading Test Total and read across from the row giving your child's Writing Total Mark.

The Key Stage 2 test level is the number shown where the row for Writing and the column for Reading intersect.

	KS2 English level *(Reading Test Total and Writing Total Mark)*

EXAMPLE

In the Reading Test Abigail scores 29.

In the Writing Test she scores 14 marks (8 for Purpose and Organisation, 3 for Grammar and 3 for Style).

She scores 11 marks in the Spelling Test and 4 marks for Handwriting, giving a Presentation Mark of 4 from the conversion table.

Adding her Presentation Mark (4) and her Writing Test Score (14) together gives a Writing Total Mark of 18.

The English test level table shows that Abigail's reading score is in the column headed 26–43. The Writing Total Mark is in the range 17–21, so the overall Key Stage 2 English test level is 4.

YOUNG AND OLD

Leo has just moved to live in a new area ... he has very few young neighbours ... he has difficulty making friends ... until he meets Gloria ... but her life is in danger ... can Leo save her?

RESCUING GLORIA

Cows would be better, thought Leo. *Or PIGS! There's no one decent living near here.* He glared through the front window of the new flat, and thought how he hated Mercy Street. How he hated the neat, sweet houses opposite with their perfect, tidy gardens. Five little ones in a terrace and a big one on the corner. The people in them were all OLD. Grannies and grandads. *Great*-grannies and great-*great*-grandads! He hadn't seen anyone under a hundred and fifty since they had moved in. He stamped angrily through the sitting room and glared at the view through his bedroom window instead. That was even worse. Even cows and pigs couldn't live in that jungle. Because his window was at the end of the block, it looked sideways, towards the big corner house next door. The house was empty, and its huge garden was a wild tangle of plants. There was no one there at *all!* Grannies or empty houses! Leo scowled at his reflection in the mirror.

Then his mum wandered into the bedroom, with baby Alice tucked under one arm and a table lamp in the other hand. 'Do you think we should put this in here? We seem to have so much *stuff*.'

Waving the lamp round vaguely, she suddenly caught sight of Leo's face and sighed.

'Cheer *up*, Leo. We've only been here three days, you know. Give it time. You'll meet plenty of people once school starts.'

'But that's six weeks!'
His mother frowned. 'Well, what about that girl downstairs? I'm sure she's about your age.'

'What girl?'

'In that flat with all the pot plants. Couldn't you make friends with her?'

'I – ' Leo wasn't sure how he felt about making friends with a strange girl. 'I might go and take a look.'

Slowly, still feeling sulky, he pulled on his best jacket and let himself out of the front door.

Quietly, because he didn't want to get caught by someone old and boring.

Once he was out in Mercy Street, he could see what his mother meant by *that flat with all the pot plants*. One of the ground-floor flats looked as though it had a forest inside. Plants crowded the windowsill, spreading thick green leaves across the glass. They climbed up the sides of the window, hung down from the top and drooped across the middle. The girl was harder to spot because she was almost hidden by plants. But she was there all right, behind the leaves, busy with a watering can. There was something brisk and business-like about her face and about the way she inspected each plant before she watered it.

Leo walked up and down a couple of times, grinning in her direction, but she didn't notice him. He even waved, but he might as well have been invisible.

Oh, that was *really* wonderful, wasn't it! At last he'd found someone his own age – and all she cared about was plants! His smile faded and he felt awkward and stupid.

Leo decided to go and explore the town. It was the holidays, after all, and people from the school must be hanging around somewhere. With a last glance at the girl – who was peering down at a weedy little plant in a yoghurt pot – he walked off up the road.

As he got to the corner, ready to turn into Grace Road, he heard a baby screaming, worse than Alice on a bad day. *I HATE this town!* he thought, for the millionth time. *There's only one thing worse than grannies, and that's BABIES. I'd like to run away to –*

He went on walking until he got to the end of Grace Road and went round the corner into the High Street. There he stopped beside a battered old Land Rover, to catch his breath. His heart thudded as if he had been running and he wanted to scream. What a fool he was! How was he *ever* going to get people to talk to him?

As he asked himself the question, he felt a sharp tug on the back of his jacket. He whirled round – and found himself looking into a pretty face with two big eyes.

Square eyes.

There was a goat in the back of the Land Rover and it had stuck its head out and taken a mouthful of his jacket.

'Hey!' Leo said. '*Hey!*'

He pulled at the jacket, but not very hard because he didn't want to tear it. The goat stared at him, in a friendly way, and clamped its teeth even tighter.

'Let go!' Leo shouted. 'Come on, you crazy goat. Let go of my jacket!'

Delicately, the goat lifted its head, pulling the jacket. There was only one way to save it from being ripped, Leo realised. He would have to take it off. Feeling rather foolish, he began to slip his arms out of the sleeves.

There was a giggle behind him

and two voices called, 'Harjinder! Harjinder!'

'Do you want any help?' said another voice. An older one that sounded friendly.

Leo looked round and saw a tall girl with long black plaits coming down the road towards him. She was carrying a heavy bag of shopping in each hand and two giggling little boys were running round her.

'Harjinder!' they shouted.

'The goat,' Leo said, feeling an idiot. 'It's got my jacket.'

He thought Harjinder would shriek with laughter, but she didn't seem a shrieking kind of person. She looked carefully at the goat and then she gave him a grin. Friendly and calm.

'Let's see if it likes this better than your jacket.'

She put her shopping down and took a paper bag full of carrots out of one of the carriers. Tipping the carrots on to the rest of the shopping she held out the paper bag.

For a second, the goat stared at her with its solemn, square eyes. Then, to Leo's amazement, it dropped his jacket and snatched at the paper bag.

'Hey, that's brilliant! What made you think of that?'

Harjinder picked up her shopping again. 'Didn't you know goats like paper?'

The bag was disappearing rapidly as the goat chewed. All Leo could do was stare.

'Why don't they get indigestion?' he said after a moment or two.

But there was no answer. Harjinder had solved his problem and gone. When he looked round, he saw her disappearing round the corner, talking busily to the two boys. He hadn't even said thank you.

Sadly, Leo scratched the lumpy top of the goat's head. 'You're the

what are you up to? Chatting up strangers?'

Leo turned and saw a very, *very* old man coming out of the nearest building. He was older than any of

only person in this whole town who's got time for me, as far as I can see.'

As the goat swallowed the last of the paper bag, he thought how pretty it was. Its coat was a pale honey colour, and everything about it was delicate: its wispy beard, its spiky eyelashes and the fine white lines down each side of its nose.

Leo went on scratching gently, and wondered why it was easier to meet goats than people in this town.

Then a voice spoke behind him. A very thick gruff voice. 'Hey, Gloria,

the people in Mercy Street, with loose brown skin that wrinkled into a thousand creases.

Gloria the goat turned towards him, snuffling her nose into his hand as he got close. He pulled gently at one of her ears.

'I wasn't hurting her,' Leo said quickly. 'Only talking to her.'

'I can tell that, boy. She likes you.' The old man took a chunk of cabbage out of his coat pocket. 'Give her this.'

Rather nervously, Leo took the cabbage and held it out. Gloria lunged forward to take a bite.

'That's it, girl,' the old man said. His voice crackled strangely. 'You have some fun while you can. You've only got another ten minutes or so.'

Leo looked at Gloria as she chewed. 'Why only ten minutes? What's going to happen then?'

Leo looked and saw that the building was a vet's. 'Is she ill?'

'She's got a bad case of motorways,' the old man said bitterly.

'Motorways?' For a second Leo wondered if it was a goat disease.

'They're building the new motorway slap-bang through my smallholding,' the old man said. 'No by-your-leave. No chance to refuse. They just sent me the money and told me I'd got to get out. Compulsory purchase, they call it.' He spat into the gutter.

'So why don't you buy somewhere else?' Leo said.

'With the money they gave me?

Not a chance. I'm going to live with my son, in his flat in Coventry.'

'A flat.' Leo looked at Gloria. It was impossible to imagine her in a flat.

'That's it.' The old man nodded. 'I can't take her. But no one else will have her either. It was easy to give away my chickens, but who wants a goat?'

Leo looked at the vet's nameplate beside the door, 'So what's going to happen to her?'

'She's going to be put to sleep,' the old man said harshly. 'I've hung on as long as I could, but I'm leaving for Coventry in two hours and that's all I can do with her.'

'Put to sleep!' Leo looked at Gloria. 'But that's dreadful!'

'Course it's dreadful.' The old man unfastened the back of the Land Rover. 'But what else can I do? Do you know a spare bit of ground where she can go and live?' He caught hold of the chain fixed to Gloria's collar and she jumped down on to the road.

'I –'

Suddenly, the words made a picture in Leo's head. The picture of the spare piece of ground that was overgrown and tangled. *Gloria could live in the wild garden next door. The one he could see from his bedroom window.*

Quickly he grabbed her chain. 'Don't go in there. I do know a place. I've got somewhere she can live!'

The old man looked at him very hard. 'Where?'

'It's –' Leo didn't want to explain exactly. 'It's where I live.'

Next... Leo has to get the goat to her new home but she has other ideas!

7

GOOD Neighbours...

It is sometimes claimed that young people and old people don't get on very well.

Susan Clarke has been finding out about an exciting link between children at a Yorkshire school and old people who live close by.

This is not true in one Yorkshire community, where elderly residents are finding that their lives are being made brighter by local children.

Class 6 of Butley Junior School are running a 'Good Neighbours' scheme, which is improving relationships with elderly people living in nearby bungalows.

The children came up with the idea themselves after complaints that thoughtless children were being noisy and dropping litter on their way to and from school.

This upset Sarah Ibison and her friends so much that they decided to go and clear up the mess, even though they hadn't dropped it! They got talking to some of the residents and things developed from there.

'We asked our teacher if we could visit some of the old people during our dinner hours,' Sarah told me.

'Soon the rest of the class heard and wanted to be involved. Our teacher helped us to contact more people and to arrange visits. Now the whole class is helping our older neighbours in lots of ways.'

Many of the old people find looking after their small gardens difficult. The children help by doing jobs such as weeding and planting bulbs. They go on errands to the local shops and even help with housework.

It isn't all work. Old and young have fun together. One of those involved, seventy-four-year-old Mrs Vera Chadwick, smiled as she told us:

'Sometimes we all sing. I've taught the children some of the songs I used to enjoy when I was young. At Christmas they bought me a Christmas tree, decorations, mince pies and a present. We enjoy talking to the young people and learning about their lives.'

Eleven-year-old Mark Brough described what the children gain:
'We talk about what life was like when they were younger and what they got up to in the old days. They make us tea and give us biscuits.'

The children have recently come up with a new 'treat' for their older friends. They take their pets on the visits too!

The headteacher of Butley Juniors, Mrs Pauline Bell, is proud of the scheme. 'This school's relationship with our neighbours is very important. We are lucky to have the senior citizens living close by. Everyone involved is developing increased understanding, and the children and the elderly feel themselves to be part of a larger, caring, considerate community.'

If the splendid efforts of these Yorkshire youngsters impress you why not set up your own 'Good Neighbours' scheme?

Dear Editor,

May I express my pleasure on reading about the 'Good Neighbours' scheme. I would like to suggest ways in which it might be extended.

The police might be pleased to set up a Home/School Watch. The old people would keep an eye on the school at night, weekends and during holidays. In return the children would keep an eye on the homes of the old people. This might reduce vandalism and the risk of break-ins.

The children are obviously respecting and valuing the Senior Citizens as members of the community and as friends.

It's really good to read about people helping others. Such unselfishness deserves praise and encouragement. The old people feel less lonely, the young more useful.

Yours sincerely,
Jane Cale
Weymouth, Dorset

Dear Sir,

I write to complain about the idea of old people being visited by children. There are several reasons why I disagree.

1 It's a lot of work for the old people. They shouldn't be expected to make tea for visitors.

2 The idea that children bring their pets to visit the elderly is silly. Animals are often dirty and can be a cause of bad health. Dogs can bring hair and mess into the homes and people may be allergic to them, causing asthma.

3 There is a danger that the children are doing so many jobs that they are taken advantage of. The children deserve a rest at lunchtime.

Yours sincerely,
Martin Skinner
Stanmore, Middlesex

TO US

OLD JOHNNY ARMSTRONG

A poem to think about...
Health, memories, friends and
visitors are just some of the
things which are important to
old people. Raymond
Wilson considers such
things in this poem.

Old Johnny Armstrong's eighty or more
And he humps like a question-mark
Over two gnarled sticks as he shuffles
and picks
His slow way to Benwell Park.

He's lived in Benwell his whole life
long
 And remembers how street-lights
 came,
  And how once on a time they
  laid a tram-line,
 Then years later dug up the
same!

 Now he's got to take a lift to his
flat,
Up where the tall winds blow
Round a Council Block that rears like a
rock
From seas of swirled traffic below.

Old Johnny Armstrong lives out his life
 In his cell on the seventeenth floor,
  And it's seldom a neighbour will do him
  a favour
   Or anyone knock at his door.

  With his poor hands knotted
   with rheumatism
   And his poor back doubled
  in pain,
  Why, day after day, should he
  pick his slow way
  To Benwell Park yet again? –

  O the wind in park trees is
  the self-same wind
  That first blew on a village
  child
  When life freshly unfurled in a
  green, lost world
  And his straight limbs ran
   wild.

11

BOOKSHELF

**Books of all kinds –
Books for all ages –
Books for a better life**

- **Land Rover 90/110 and Defender Owner's Workshop Manual**
  Authors: Steve Rendle and Mark Combs
  Publisher: Haynes
  'The classic do-it-yourself motorguide'

- **The Complete Book of Mother and Baby Care**
  Author: Elizabeth Fenwick
  Publisher: Dorling Kindersley
  'Everything the title claims'

- **Dimanche Diller**
  Author: Henrietta Branford
  Publisher: Young Lions
  'A pacey page-turner of an adventure story'

- **The Houseplant Survival Manual**
  Author: William Davidson
  Publisher: Ward Lock
  'The complete guide to indoor gardening'

- **Amber Brown's Not a Crayon**
  Author: Paula Danziger
  Publisher: Young Piper
  'A brilliantly funny, sad and readable story about a once-in-a-lifetime friendship'

- **The New Goat Handbook**
  Author: Ulrich
  Publisher: Barras
  'All you need to know to keep your goat healthy – ideal for beginners'

- **Woof**
  Author: Alan Snow
  Publisher: Doubleday
  'A simple, amusing story about a lively, dotty dog. Ideal for babies learning to handle books'

- **Breakfast in the Ruins**
  Author: Michael Moorcock
  Publisher: Phoenix House
  'Classic adult science fiction fantasy – strong story, strong characters'

Extract from 'Rescuing Gloria' by Gillian Cross reproduced by kind permission of the publishers, Methuen Children's Books.

Poem 'Old Johnny Armstrong' by Raymond Wilson, from 'Old and New: Poems to Enjoy' by James Gibson and Raymond Wilson, reproduced by kind permission of the publishers, John Murray.

First published 1995
New edition 1995

Letts Educational
Aldine House
Aldine Place
London W12 8AW
Telephone: 0181 743 7514

Text: © John Lisle

Design and illustrations: © BPP (Letts Educational) Ltd 1995

British Library Cataloguing in Publication Data

A CIP record for this book is available from the British Library.

ISBN 1 85758 435 X

Printed in Great Britain by W. M. Print, Ltd., Walsall, West Midlands WS2 29E

Letts Educational is the trading name of BPP (Letts Educational) Ltd